P9-ANZ-156

ALSO BY
FRANCES O'ROARK DOWELL

Frances O'Roark Dowell

how to BUILD a STORY...

illustrated by Stacy Ebert

or, THE BIG WHAT IF

A CAITLYN DLOUHY BOOK

ATHENEUM BOOKS FOR YOUNG READERS

New York   London   Toronto   Sydney   New Delhi

ATHENEUM BOOKS FOR YOUNG READERS • An imprint of Simon & Schuster Children's Publishing Division • 1230 Avenue of the Americas, New York, New York 10020 • This book is a work of fiction. Any references to historical events, real people, or real places are used fictitiously. Other names, characters, places, and events are products of the author's imagination, and any resemblance to actual events or places or persons, living or dead, is entirely coincidental. • Text copyright © 2020 by Frances O'Roark Dowell • Illustrations copyright © 2020 by Stacy Ebert • All rights reserved, including the right of reproduction in whole or in part in any form. • ATHENEUM BOOKS FOR YOUNG READERS is a registered trademark of Simon & Schuster, Inc. Atheneum logo is a trademark of Simon & Schuster, Inc. • For information about special discounts for bulk purchases, please contact Simon & Schuster Special Sales at 1-866-506-1949 or business@simonandschuster.com. • The Simon & Schuster Speakers Bureau can bring authors to your live event. For more information or to book an event, contact the Simon & Schuster Speakers Bureau at 1-866-248-3049 or visit our website at www.simonspeakers.com. • Jacket design by Debra Sfetsios-Conover; interior design by Irene Metaxatos • The text for this book was set in Guardi LT Std. • The illustrations for this book were rendered with traditional and digital pencil and then digitally painted in Photoshop using a Wacom tablet. • Manufactured in the United States of America • 0620 BVG • First Edition • 10 9 8 7 6 5 4 3 2 1 • Library of Congress Cataloging-in-Publication Data • Names: Dowell, Frances O'Roark, author. • Title: How to build a story . . . or, the big what if / Frances O'Roark Dowell. • Description: First edition. | New York : Atheneum Books for Young Readers, [2020] | "A Caitlyn Dlouhy Book" | Audience: Ages 10 up | Audience: Grades 4–6 | Summary: "An instructional book on how to write a story from bestselling author Frances O'Roark Dowell"—Provided by publisher. • Identifiers: LCCN 2019023000 | ISBN 9781534438422 (hardback) | ISBN 9781534438446 (eBook) • Subjects: LCSH: Authorship—Juvenile literature. | Storytelling—Juvenile literature. | Fiction—Authorship—Juvenile literature. • Classification: LCC PN159.D69 2020 | DDC 808.02—dc23 • LC record available at https://lccn.loc.gov/2019023000

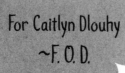

For Caitlyn Dlouhy
~F. O. D.

To Joshua, J. R.
Samuel, and Noah —
building a story with
you is my favorite

~S. E.

HELLO and Welcome to My Book About Writing!

I'M REALLY GLAD YOU'RE HERE. Do you have a second to chat? You do? Fantastic!

Okay, let me say this as simply as I can: a writer is someone who writes. Period. You don't have to publish what you write to be a writer. You don't need a degree, a certificate, or a license. You don't need anybody's permission or to follow anybody else's rules. You don't even have to be that good at it. All you have to do to be a writer is write.

Have you ever written anything? A poem about your brother's weird toes? A paragraph describing the best way to make a peanut-butter-and-marshmallow-fluff sandwich? Four pages of a novel about life on Planet Wonko?

Okay then—you're a writer.

Are you constantly coming up with story ideas, making lists of great character names, scribbling scenes in notebooks?

Excellent. You've come to the right book.

Maybe you're one of those people who hate to write. Maybe writing a story or a paper or a three-sentence

paragraph makes you feel like you're taking a bath in a vat of bumblebees and vinegar. Maybe the very idea of writing makes your insides shrivel up like a worm on a hot sidewalk.

You also have come to the right book.

I started writing when I was a kid. I wrote lots of poems and the beginnings of novels (I always gave up after seven or eight pages). I never thought of myself as a writer, but I wrote all the time, which is how I eventually ended up writing books like *Dovey Coe*, *Falling In*, and *Phineas L. MacGuire . . . Erupts!* Maybe you've read one of my books. If not, I'll pause here while you run to the library and check a few of them out.

[Pauses. Waits for reader to go to the library.]

Oh, you're back. Good!

So here's the thing: after I'd published a bunch of books, I started teaching writing workshops for kids. Some kids come to these workshops because they love to write. Others come because their parents make them. As a teacher, I want to make my enthusiastic students even more enthusiastic about writing poems and stories. My less enthusiastic students? I want them to learn that everybody has a story to tell and can find the words to tell it. At the very least, I want to make the writing process a little less painful. Two-thirds less painful. Okay, 37 percent less painful.

This is a book for writers. It's a book for writers who love to write and writers who like to write and for writers who hate to write. I don't know about you, but that describes me to a T. I love writing, I like writing, I hate writing. I find writing easy, hard, exciting, and boring.

But even on the days when I'm bored, or everything I write sounds dumb, I stick with it. Bad days are most often followed by good ones, and weird as it sounds, sometimes boredom is what gets you to the exciting stuff. Whatever kind of writing day I'm having, I always remember that every time I sit down to write, I get to make up new worlds. I get to create people out of thin air. I get to write the story I've always wanted to read.

Who else gets to do all that?

You!

Now, before we get on with the show, I want to share something very important with you. Sometimes I find that younger writers (and some older ones, too) have unrealistic expectations about what's going to happen when they sit down to write a story. I think this is one reason some kids decide early on that they're bad writers and shouldn't even try. So I've made a short list of things I think are true for all writers, from the most experienced to the absolute beginner. I call this list . . .

5 THINGS I KNOW FOR SURE ABOUT WRITING

1. FIRST DRAFTS ARE THE WORST DRAFTS.

You have a great idea for a story, but when you sit down to write this amazing, entertaining, brilliant epic—well, you can't get the words to come out right. In fact, it seems like the words aren't saying what you want them to say at all! It's like you're thinking, *Come on words, work with me here!* And the words are all watching Netflix and eating nachos.

So frustrating! In your mind, you see the image of a thousand black stallions thundering across the moonlit plains, the Dark Lord of the Cosmos at the lead. But when you try to transfer this image into words, you come up with something like *The black horses ran fast and were really loud. Lord Moribund's horse was also really fast and loud. He was in the front.*

Somehow this lacks the poetry of your original vision. It's tempting to delete it (or tear it out of your notebook). Don't! Your job right now is to put your story into words, however lame those words might sound. Think of it this way: when you're writing a story, you're creating something that didn't exist until you made it up and wrote it down. In a way, you're creating something out of nothing. And you know what? That's hard work.

2. IT'S NOT JUST YOU – ALL WRITERS STRUGGLE TO GET IT RIGHT

Think about your favorite book, the book you've reread at least ten times, possibly ten million. Ponder the many reasons you love it. Then wrap your brain around the fact that this book—the absolute best book ever written on Planet Earth— started out as a worst first draft. Full of clunky sentences. Poorly described settings. Boring characters. Not only that, the author who wrote this book likely has drawers full of other books that have never seen the light of day, that's how bad they are. She has piles of stories that fall apart halfway through.

She has written sentences that make her cringe to think about. (Okay, it's possible that I'm talking about myself here. But I know lots and lots of other writers, and most of them also have at least one drawer full of, well, future compost.)

My point is this: all writers struggle to say what they want to say the way they want to say it. It's not just you, it's not just me. Sure, we writers have our good days when the words flow and we astonish ourselves with our brilliance, but we have just as many days when we feel like tearing our hair out. The next time you see a picture of your favorite writer, look for the bald patches. And then get back to work.

3. EVERY WRITER NEEDS AN EDITOR.

We think of writing as a solo activity, and to some extent it is. When you're writing a draft, it's you and your computer (or your pen and notebook). But having someone else read what you've written and give you feedback is an absolutely essential part of the process. *You* know what you're trying to say, but you need a reader to let you know if you've actually *said* what you meant. You also need someone who can tell you what you've left out of your story and what you *should* have left out.

This person is called an editor. Every book you've ever loved had an editor, and the editor played a very important role in making that book one you read time and time again. Editors don't just correct mistakes. They also make suggestions. Sometimes they'll throw out a few ideas for different directions your story might take. They won't write your story for you (no matter how much you beg them to), but they will help you make it a lot better.

4. WRITING MEANS REVISING.

So. Let's accept the idea that our first drafts will be our worst drafts and that we need someone to give us feedback so we can write a much better second draft. You with me? We've all agreed to accept this? Fabulous!

It's harder to accept the fact that a third draft may be required.

Maybe even a fourth.

I'm sorry to have to tell you that.

The good news is that each revision is a little easier to do than the one before. By the time you get to that third (or fourth or fifth) (sorry, sorry!) draft, you're no longer making huge changes. You're finessing. You're adding a scene here or a description there to make your story richer, your plot more compelling.

And fear not: at some point the revisions end. You've done all that you can do. This isn't the same as saying your story is perfect. It's just as close to perfect as you can get it. And that's perfect enough.

5. WRITING IS LIKE A SPORT: IT TAKES PRACTICE TO GET GOOD.

Every spring my gym offers a "Couch to 5K" class for out-of-shape people who want to get in shape. That would be me. We start off slow—maybe two laps around the track—and over time we build up our endurance, so by the end of the class six weeks later we can run three miles. Maybe three very slow miles (that would be me again), but three miles all the same. Some people who take this class end up running marathons. (That, in case you were wondering, would *not* be me.) Others of us never run another race in our lives, but we leave the class in much better shape than we started.

Either way, we former couch potatoes were able to meet our goal—running in a 5K—by practicing every day and building our endurance a little bit at a time.

If you want to be a better runner, run every day.

If you want to be a better writer, write every day.

Now, if you don't like to write, this sounds like t-o-r-t-u-r-e. My advice to you is to start slow. Get a journal and write for five minutes a day for the first week, build up to ten minutes the second week, and keep adding minutes until you're up to twenty minutes a day. Write about *anything*. Write about your favorite team's chances to win its division or how your sister stole the last brownie, the one that you'd wrapped up in a napkin with the word "POISON" written on it. Write about your dog, how he hides under the couch when he knows he's about to be put in his crate. Write about that kid you only ever see in the cafeteria, even though she's in your grade. Where does she hide out for the rest of the day?

Write a story that you add to a little bit every day. It doesn't matter what you write about—it just matters that you spend time every day writing.

Why do this? Because the more you practice writing, the easier it gets. The blank screen or page is a lot less scary once you know that filling it up isn't a big deal. And you might even find that when you write about things you're interested in, you'll actually enjoy yourself.

If you love to write, then think of yourself as an athlete training for a big game. Serious athletes work out every day, listen to their coaches, and eat to win. Serious writers write every day, get feedback from their editors, and read. They read a lot.

If you love to write, daily writing practice will be a way for you to experiment with different kinds of writing, work on the parts of writing you find difficult (say, description or dialogue), or just have fun. If you're working on a novel and add a few paragraphs or pages daily, you'll have a completed draft before you know it. Think of the writers, artists, athletes, and musicians you love the most. How did they get where they are today? Yeah, you know the answer—practice, practice, practice. Talent is only a small part of what makes someone successful. Putting in the hours is what really does the trick.

Those are the Big Five, the things about writing I know for sure. Except I think maybe I left one extremely important thing out: writing can be tons of fun. And you know what? Sometimes a miracle happens and your first draft actually comes out pretty good. And when you're working on a story you love, it's almost impossible to stop, even if you're about to collapse into an exhausted heap.

You ready to get started? Fabulous! Fantastic!

Let's do this.

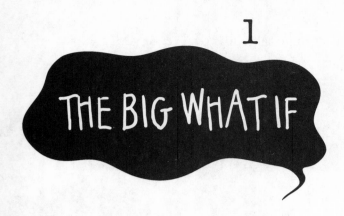

1

THE BIG WHAT IF

SO HOW DO WE GET THIS STORY STARTED? Where do we begin? How do we fill up alllllll those blank pages?

Simple! We start with a question. It's called **The Big What If**.

What if you woke up one morning and realized you could fly?

What if it turns out the new kid in your class is actually a ghost, and she doesn't seem to like you very much?

What if a bilingual family starts a friendly contest to see who can go the longest without speaking English?

What if a girl's dog went missing for several days, and when she finally finds him she discovers he has a whole other family?

The easiest way to start writing a story is to make a list of what-if questions and then pick one. Flip that question into a statement, and you've got the beginning of your story.

What if I woke up one morning and realized I could fly?
becomes
One morning I woke up and realized I could fly.

What if a girl's dog went missing for several days, and when she finally finds him she discovers he has a whole other family?

becomes

A girl's dog goes missing for several days, and when she finally finds him she discovers he has a whole other family.

The what-if question gives you the two things you need to begin a story: a character and a situation.

Let's give this a try. I like the idea of the girl searching for her dog and discovering that he has a second family. So how can we get this party started?

How about something like this:

The sirens screamed in the distance, and Olivia knew
that if she didn't move fast, she and Max would be
trapped in the Schiffers' front yard, with all those whiny,
weirdo Schiffer kids pointing at her like she was some
dog thief. But she wasn't a thief—Max belonged to her,
not those horrible, terrible, no-good Schiffers!

It only took a second to scoop Max up and zoom to
the street, the wails of the littlest Schiffers chasing
them all the way down the block. Olivia had practically
hit warp speed and was taking off into the stratosphere
when someone flicked the switch on the sirens and
everything went quiet. Slowing down to the slowest
of sprints, with Max panting in her ear, Olivia looked
around. No police anywhere. Had they really been after
her in the first place?

Maybe, maybe not, but at least she'd gotten Max
away from those horrible Schiffers!

"I've got to sit down, pup," she said before collapsing
onto the curb. "I'm too pooped to scoot one step farther.
Besides, you and me need to have a chat. You've
disappeared three times in the last month, and a bunch
of times before that. What's up? Don't you know how
scared I get when you run away? If you're not careful,
some other family is going to snatch you up."

Olivia stopped. Her brain was circling around a

thought like a monkey going after a weasely weasel.

"Max!" she gasped. "The Schiffers said you were their dog—and they seemed pretty serious. Do you have a second family, Max?"

She paused again, another terrible thought dawning on her. "Or are we your second family? Who did you belong to before we rescued you? What's the story here?"

Max, being a dog, didn't reply, but he did give Olivia a look that sent chills down her brain plate all the way to her tiniest toenails.

So Olivia goes looking for her dog and realizes he has another family—and not only that, she's afraid that the other family might be the one Max belonged to first. If that's the case, does she have to give him up?

So there you have it: the beginning of a story! If I want to know what happens next, I'll have to keep writing it.

Here's what I want you to notice. I don't dump a lot of information into this opening. I don't tell you how old Olivia is or what she looks like or how many brothers and sisters she has. That information might be important, but it can wait.

Instead of opening the story with lots of information, I start it with **somebody doing something**. I start with action. I get things going right away, which is what you should do, too. Throw your protagonist into the pool!

Make her fall off her skateboard and roll into a deep, dark hole. He's giving a knock-kneed speech and drops all of his notecards. She looks into the mirror and discovers she's invisible. No preambles, no big explanations, nothing but net. Game on, baby!

Okay, I'll stop now.

Let's get back to the flying boy and see what's going on with him.

This morning I woke up and realized I could fly.

The morning started out the same as every morning. The first thing I did was smash the clock-radio alarm with my fist so it would stop making that terrible racket, and then I slowly put my feet on the floor. I sat like that for a second, the way I always do, until I finally forced myself to stand up.

Only this morning I didn't exactly stand up. I flew up. It was the weirdest thing. One second I'm sitting on the side of my bed, the next second I'm up on the ceiling.

"Josh, your cereal's getting soggy," my mom called from the kitchen. "Hurry up and get down here."

I tried to fly to the ground so I could walk downstairs, but I couldn't do it. So I flew to the kitchen. When my mom saw me, she started screaming, which freaked me out so bad, I flew to the front door and out of the house. And then I just kept flying.

Again, I start this story with somebody doing something—in this case, flying out of bed. Josh doesn't know why he can fly, he just can. The question is, where will he fly to and what kind of trouble is he going to get in?

Which brings us to one of the most important things you want to do in the beginning of your story. **You want to make your reader supercurious about what happens next.** You want your reader to turn the page.

Okay, let's do an End-of-the-Chapter Wrap-up for those of you keeping score at home.

FIRST: THE BIG TAKE-HOME

- All you need to start a story is a character and a situation. The beauty of the what-if question is that it gives you both.
- Open your story with somebody doing something.
- Make your reader want to know what happens next.

NEXT: WRITERS, START YOUR ENGINES!

1. Make a what-if list. Try to come up with at least ten what-if statements, from the everyday and mundane to the very weird and fantastical.
2. Review your list. Pick the what-if question that interests you the most.
3. Flip that what-if question and make it a statement.

FINALLY: LET'S WRITE!

1. Open your story with an action scene that sets up your protagonist's situation. To write this opening scene, pretend you're making a movie. The camera pans in on your protagonist as he's . . . doing what? Jumping up and down on a trampoline? Rushing through breakfast because he's late for the bus? Putting on her space suit? Getting chased by a dog?
2. Whatever it is, your character's doing it, and

then suddenly . . . something happens! He runs blindly toward the bus and runs smack into a bear! A UFO lands on the sidewalk in front of her! He steps into the spaceship and it takes off—without the other astronauts! She waves her wand and the whole world disappears!

You get the picture. Write a scene that gets the story going and makes your reader eager to know what happens next!

THE PROTAGONIST

Protago-what? If this is a new one for you, let me explain . . . In this chapter, we met two characters: Olivia and Josh. They're the main characters in their stories, the stars of their shows.

We call a story's main character the *protagonist.* Some famous protagonists include Harry Potter, Spider-Man, Ramona Quimby, Melody Brooks, Junie B. Jones, Alvin Ho, and Josh and Jordon Bell.

Other terms for *protagonist* include *hero, central character,* and *lead character.*

The word *protagonist* comes from two Greek words— *protos,* which means "first in importance," and *agonistes,* which means "actor." So *protagonist* essentially means the most important actor in the story.

2

The BACKGROUND CHECK

OPEN YOUR STORY WITH AN ACTION SCENE. Draw your reader in. And then tell your reader a few things she needs to know before you continue. What's your story's setting? When does it take place? What does your reader need to know about your main character for the rest of the story to make sense?

I call this part of the story the **Background Check**.

The background check lets your reader know a little bit about your protagonist and what life is like for them as the story begins. For instance, near the beginning of *Harry Potter and the Sorcerer's Stone*, Harry goes into the kitchen and sees all of his cousin's birthday presents, including a bike (which Harry thinks is odd, since Dudley doesn't exercise voluntarily). Following his train of thought, we learn some very interesting things about Harry's background: he lives in a cupboard under the stairs of his aunt and uncle's house, and he looks especially small and skinny because he wears oversized hand-me-downs.

We also learn something very important about his past:

his parents died in a car accident when Harry was a baby, an accident that left him with a lightning-bolt-shaped scar on his forehead.

That's some useful information to have as the story unfolds.

Let's return to Olivia and Max from a few pages ago. We already know some things about Olivia from the opening scene, or we can at least make some educated guesses, right? We assume she's a tween or a young teen—old enough to go out looking for her missing dog on her own, but not so old that she's driving a car. She's old enough to make an interesting deduction about why Max keeps running away (maybe the Schiffers are his original owners and he keeps going back to them), but young enough to find the Schiffer kids totally annoying. An older teenager might be more sympathetic about how distressed the Schiffers are about someone taking their dog—in fact, an older teenager might have asked to talk to their parents instead of just snatching Max away.

We learn that the Schiffers aren't strangers to Olivia—she knows their last name and seems to generally dislike them.

Is there anything else we need to know about Olivia before the story continues?

It might be good to know exactly how old she is. There's a big difference between being in fifth grade and being in eighth. Ten- or eleven-year-old Olivia is going to react to whatever happens next differently than fourteen-year-old Olivia, and she'd going to come up with a different plan.

Other useful pieces of info: How long has Olivia's family had Max? What time of year is it—is it the middle of winter or summer break? Finally, given how irritating Olivia finds the Schiffer children, does she have some sort of history with them? The background check might be a place to let your reader know why Olivia has a beef with these kids.

Okay, let's do a background check on Olivia. Here's the first section again:

> The sirens screamed in the distance, and Olivia knew that if she didn't move fast, she and Max would be trapped in the Schiffers' front yard, with all those whiny, weirdo Schiffer kids pointing at her like she was some dog thief. But she wasn't a thief—Max belonged to her, not those horrible, terrible, no-good Schiffers!
>
> It only took a second to scoop Max up and zoom to the street, the wails of the littlest Schiffers chasing them all the way down the block. Olivia had practically hit warp speed and was taking off into the stratosphere when someone flicked the switch on the sirens and everything went quiet. Slowing down to the slowest of sprints, with Max panting in her ear, Olivia looked around. No police anywhere. Had they really been after her in the first place?
>
> Maybe, maybe not, but at least she'd gotten Max away from those horrible Schiffers!
>
> "I've got to sit down, pup," she said before collapsing

onto the curb. "I'm too pooped to scoot one step farther. Besides, you and me need to have a chat. You've disappeared three times in the last month. What's up with that? Don't you know how scared I get when you run away? If you're not careful, some other family is going to snatch you up."

Olivia stopped. Her brain was circling around a thought like a monkey going after a weasely weasel. "Max!" she gasped. "The Schiffers said you were their dog—and they seemed pretty serious. Do you have a second family, Max?"

She paused again, another terrible thought dawning on her. "Or are we your second family? Who did you belong to before we rescued you? What's the story here?"

Max, being a dog, didn't reply, but he did give Olivia a look that sent chills down her brain plate all the way to her tiniest toenails.

Now how about we add a little background info?

Olivia struggled to her feet, clutching Max to her chest. Maybe the police weren't chasing her, but what if those stupid Schiffer kids were? She'd better get home—they didn't know where she lived, did they? No, during the school year the bus picked up Olivia first in the morning and dropped her off last in the afternoon. Every morning from September through June, she got a front-row view of the screeching, squabbling Schiffers as the bus pulled up to the curb in front of their house, which was twice as nice as Olivia's, or at least twice as big. Everybody knows they're rich, Olivia thought as she quickened her pace. They could buy another dog if they want one so badly—they don't need Max. Besides, they obviously don't care about him, or else how did he end up at the pound last January, skinny and shivering?

Well, she was going to make sure the Schiffers couldn't find Max even if they did figure out where Olivia lived. She'd build a fort in the woods behind her house and camp out there all summer. Her parents wouldn't care—they worked ninety hours a day—and her brother was spending all summer at a sleepaway camp for computer geeks. Nope, now that Olivia was twelve and could take care of herself, she could do whatever she wanted. And what she wanted to do was to keep Max away from the Schiffers.

Notice that I didn't tell you everything in the world about Olivia in this section, but I did give you some important information. You know she's twelve, she's got a brother, and her parents work too much to pay a lot of attention to her. You know her family adopted Max earlier in the year, and he was in bad shape when they got him. She doesn't seem to have a *specific* beef with the Schiffers, but she doesn't seem to like them very much. Whatever happens next, having this information about Olivia will help you understand the reasons for her actions and reactions as the story goes on.

Okay, let's take a second to check in with Josh, our flying boy.

This morning I woke up and realized I could fly.

The morning started out the same as every morning. The first thing I did was smash the clock-radio alarm with my fist so it would stop making that terrible racket, and then I slowly put my feet on the floor. I sat like that for a second, the way I always do, until I finally forced myself to stand up.

Only this morning I didn't exactly stand up. I flew up. It was the weirdest thing. One second I'm sitting on the side of my bed, the next second I'm on the ceiling.

"Josh, your cereal's getting soggy," my mom called from the kitchen. "Hurry up and get down here."

I tried to fly to the ground so I could walk downstairs, but I couldn't do it. So I flew to the kitchen. When my mom saw me, she started screaming, which freaked me out so bad, I flew to the front door and out of the house. And then I just kept flying.

So that first section gets the story off the ground—now what do we need to better understand Josh's actions and reactions as the story continues?

Background check: One thing you should know about me: My life is pretty boring. I live in a medium-size house, and I have a little sister who's a medium pain in the butt. Every day is the same—I get up, I get ready for school, go to school, come home, blah blah blah. My parents are nice, but their idea of a good time is sitting next to each other on the couch playing solitaire on their laptops. I'm okay at sports, get okay grades, have an okay number of friends. You get the picture.

We get the picture—waking up to discover he can fly is a big, weird, exciting deal for Josh. It's not the least bit normal. It would be a different story entirely if Josh told us he came from a family of flyers. If that were the case, then discovering he could fly might have been exciting for Josh, but it wouldn't have come as a complete surprise.

What else do we learn from this short background check? The story takes place around now—Josh's parents have laptops. Josh's family isn't rich or poor. He has a little sister and takes the bus to school.

As a writer, you don't want your readers feeling confused or frustrated. You don't want them to get halfway through your story and suddenly realize that it takes place on another planet or in a fantasy world or two hundred years ago. That's why including the background check in the early pages of your story is important.

All right then, let's wrap things up!

THE BIG TAKE-HOME

⊸ The second section of your story should give your reader background information about your protagonist, the story's setting, and the time in which the story takes place.

⊸ The background check lets your reader know what normal life is like for your protagonist.

WRITERS, START YOUR ENGINES!

1. Get to know your protagonist. The protagonist (in case you weren't listening the first time I brought this up) is your main character, your lead actor, the person who finds him- or herself in The Big-What-If situation. In order to proceed with your story, you need to know a few things about your protagonist and his or her circumstances. Why don't you take a few minutes to sketch out some details?

   Background:
   ⊸ Name and age
   ⊸ Setting and time (examples: Mars, two thousand years in the future; or suburbs outside of big city, now)
   ⊸ Family background (examples: parents, siblings, country of origin if important, etc.)
   ⊸ Friend group
   ⊸ Important personal facts (examples: orphaned, incredibly wealthy, very poor, has disability or special

abilities, has experienced recent trauma such as death in the family or of a close friend, a missing pet, a car accident, a big loss of some sort)

↬ Character traits (remember, your protagonist can and should have positive and negative traits): outgoing shy fearless nervous generally happy generally unhappy unreliable generous loyal patient impatient kind sincere insincere insecure self-controlled

undisciplined determined unsure adventurous
homebody fair selfish dishonest disloyal unkind
greedy quarrelsome playful silly wild reckless
stubborn funny rough talkative grounded disciplined

What else can you come up with? Go wild—now's the time to put that incredible imagination of yours to work!

2. What does your protagonist want most of all? To be loved? To be feared? To fit in? To find his cat? To win the big race? To exact revenge on her enemy? To win the undying affection of his one true love?

LET'S WRITE!

You've already written an opening scene—congratulations! See, it wasn't that hard, was it? Clearly you've got what it takes to do this story-writing thing. Now let's take it to the next level and include some background information about your character and the setting. The background check might just be a paragraph long, or it might be a complete scene in which your protagonist has a flashback to an earlier event in her life.

Piece of cake, right? Now write!

3

The BIG PROBLEM

HEY, LOOK AT WHAT YOU'VE ALREADY ACCOMPLISHED! You've got a character and you've got a situation. You've given your reader a little background information on your story's setting and protagonist. Now what you need is a problem. A big problem.

This is a must-have, a non-negotiable, a total deal-breaker. **If your main character doesn't have a problem, then you don't have a story.**

Take a look at Josh the flying boy. If he just spends a few hours flying around his neighborhood and comes back home, well, okay, that's sort of interesting. But is it a story? Sort of, kind of.

But not really. Not a great story, anyway.

Because why? (You know this!)

Because it doesn't have a big problem.

But try this on for size: What if Josh flew out his front door, met up with a flock of birds, had a great time flying around . . . and then realized he was being followed by a drone?

And that drone was trying to make him fall out of the sky?

Now we're talking.

Now we've got ourselves a **Big Problem**!

The big problem is the problem that the character has to solve by the time the story ends.

The big problem can be really dramatic (your protagonist has been kidnapped and is being held for ransom), or a

little less life-or-death (your protagonist sends her best friend a text that comes off offensive instead of funny, and her best friend dumps her). Whatever kind of problem it is, the big problem has to propel your character into action. The problem must be solved!

Let's look at some examples from some stories you're probably familiar with. You remember Wilbur the pig from *Charlotte's Web*, right? What's Wilbur's problem? Once Farmer Zuckerman fattens him up, Wilber is going to be turned into a ham.

That's a big problem.

Did you ever read *Hatchet* by Gary Paulsen? Remember what happens to the main character, Brian? The small plane he's flying in crashes, and he finds himself alone in the wilderness, with only a hatchet and his wits to survive.

Big problem.

Sometimes the big problem comes in the form of a mystery that needs to be solved or a question that needs to be answered. In *The Parker Inheritance* by Varian Johnson, Candice finds a letter filled with clues that could lead her to a buried treasure and the truth about her grandmother. But if she can't decipher those clues, well, forget the treasure and the truth.

Noah's quest in *Flush* is to answer two questions: Is the casino boat that's docked in the town harbor flushing raw sewage into the water, and if so, how is it getting away with such a dastardly deed?

So what's our girl Olivia's big problem? This one's pretty straightforward: her beloved dog just might belong to some-one else. Not only that, she thinks the original owners neglected the dog (which is why he showed up at the shelter half-starved and shivering), and she can't bear the thought of giving him back.

There are some stories, like Olivia's, where the problem comes up almost immediately, and other stories, like Josh's, where it might take a page or two for the big problem to rear its ugly head. The big problem doesn't have to pop up right away, but keep in mind that you don't want to go too long before introducing it, or your reader might lose interest.

One thing you need to make sure of: that your reader understands what the consequences are for your main char-acter if the big problem isn't solved.

If the kidnapped guy's parents don't pay his ransom, he's getting dumped in the ocean.

If the girl who sent the offensive text doesn't win her friend back, she'll have to eat lunch alone for the rest of year, maybe the rest of her life.

It's important for you as the writer to understand the con-sequences, too, of course. Knowing the consequences will help you better understand your protagonist's motivations and actions as he or she sets off on the bumpy road that leads to the end of the story.

Finally, you don't have to know how the problem will be solved when you begin writing the story. Some writers start

their stories knowing how things work out in the end, others don't. You may surprise yourself by writing a story with an ending that you never expected!

You know what time it is, right? It's Wrap-up Time!

THE BIG TAKE-HOME

- ∽ For a story to be a story, it needs three things: A main character, a situation, and a problem that arises from the situation that has to be solved.
- ∽ The problem can be a life-and-death matter, or something less dire (a lost homework assignment, a misunderstanding between friends), but either way, it has to propel your character into action.

- You can introduce the problem immediately or build up to it—but don't take too long to get to it, or else your reader may lose interest.
- Both you and your reader need to understand what the consequences are for your main character if the big problem isn't solved.

WRITERS, START YOUR ENGINES!

What is your character's big problem? If it's not obvious to you, try some brainstorming. Make a list of possible problems, and don't be afraid of getting too crazy! For example, what if there's an unfriendly ghost in your protagonist's classroom? Possible big problems include:

1. Unfriendly ghost wants your protagonist out of the picture and keeps causing hazardous accidents in the gym and the chemistry lab.
2. Unfriendly ghost has plans to ruin the school dance, which your protagonist has been looking forward to all year.
3. Unfriendly ghost keeps stealing your protagonist's homework, and your protagonist is on the verge of flunking math as a result.
4. Unfriendly ghost has plans to turn everyone in the class into zombies.
5. Unfriendly ghost is part of a ghost army that's trying to take over the world.

6. Unfriendly ghost is really former Italian dictator Benito Mussolini and wants to turn the class into a fascist regime.

7. Unfriendly ghost won't stop singing "The Wheels on the Bus" in your protagonist's ear.

8. Unfriendly ghost isn't really a ghost at all, but a projected computer image created to make your protagonist go crazy.

Okay, your turn. Start brainstorming!

LET'S WRITE!

There are several ways (maybe dozens!) to introduce your protagonist's big problem. Try one of the following:

- **Write a scene in which your protagonist slowly realizes he has a problem.** When the scene starts, your character is quite happy (think of Josh having a great time flying around his neighborhood), but then something happens (hello, drone!), and your character realizes that he's in trouble.

- **Write a scene in which the problem is introduced suddenly.** Sometimes a story begins with a crisis (Olivia finds her runaway dog with another family), and your protagonist has to act quickly (as Olivia does when she grabs Max and runs toward home).

- **Write a scene in which your protagonist learns she has a problem during a conversation.** Sasha gets on the bus and starts chatting with her best friend, who's being strangely quiet. "What's wrong with you?" she finally asks, and her friend says, "Nothing, I'm just worried about the big test today." Your protagonist feels confused. Test? What test? Uh-oh.

AVOID CLICHÉS
LIKE THE PLAGUE

When you're writing dramatic scenes—such as the introduction of a story's big problem—it can be easy to fall back on clichés, phrases that are so overused and overdone that they don't feel the least bit fresh. Here are just a few:

Eyes that twinkle. Eyes that shine. Smiles that light up a room. Bellies like bowls full of jelly. Feet as big as gun boats.

People who are mad as wet hens, mad as hatters, crazy as loons, hungry as horses, hungry as wolves, hungry as bears, tired as one-armed paper hangers.

A character who's like a kid in a candy store. A good listener who's all ears or a surprised guy who can't believe his ears or grins from ear to ear. A beloved child who's the apple of her parents' eye or who has eyes bigger than her stomach. A killer who doesn't bat an eye, a grandmother who's blind as a bat.

You get my point.

Here's a fun exercise: see how many clichés you can come up with! Make a list of at least fifty—and then keep that list with you whenever you're writing, so you know exactly what sort of descriptions to avoid.

4

WHAT'S THE PLAN?

WARNING: WE'RE ABOUT TO ENTER DANGEROUS TERRITORY, otherwise known as the middle of the story.

(Cue mass stampede toward exit, screaming writers dumping their notebooks into huge trash cans as they attempt to flee to safety.)

Maybe this has happened to you. You have a great idea for a story, and when you start writing you can hardly keep up with your thoughts, they're coming so fast. You write an amazing opening scene, go into some background details, move the story forward with the big problem . . . and then everything goes black. The brakes squeal and the wheels griiiiiiiind to a halt. You look around and find yourself in the middle of a desert, without a single thought or good idea to your name.

This is where a lot of writers quit. Most of us have drawers filled with unfinished stories—stories that came fast out of the gate and then ran out of steam. Stories we were having so much fun writing—until we weren't.

So what do we do about the problem of the middle? For most writers I know, the middle of a story is the hardest part

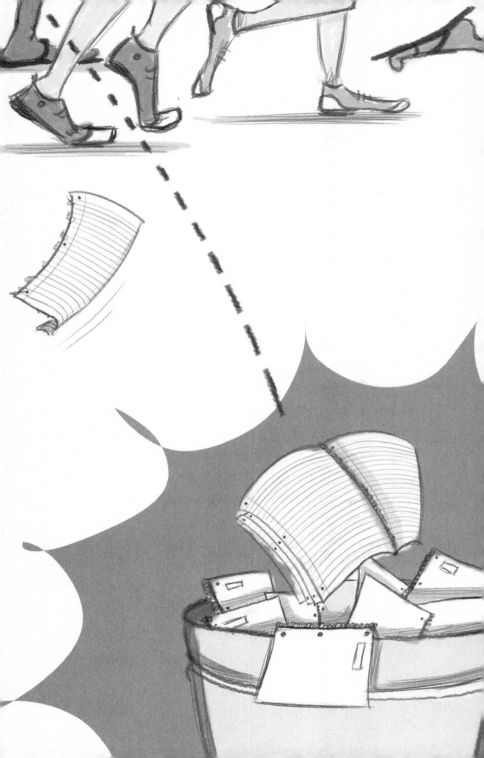

to write. You've given your protagonist a big problem, and you may even have an idea of how she'll get that problem solved. But how do you get from here to there?

This is a good time to talk about how your character is on a journey.

A journey has a beginning, and it has an end.

It's the miles between the two that make up most of the journey, and sometimes those miles seem impossible to get across. Writing middles can be daunting, but keep in mind that the middle is where most of the good stuff happens. It's where friendships grow, unexpected allies show up, clues are uncovered, and people get lost and found or find themselves eating with the weirdest kid in the cafeteria or meeting up with the minions of the Dark Lord. Plots get hatched and thwarted in the middle; victories both small and large are won, defeats are suffered. A lot happens in the middle of a story, the way a lot happens in the middle of a sandwich—you've got your peanut butter and your marshmallow fluff, you've got your layer of crushed potato chips . . . or is that just my sandwich? Anyway, what I'm trying to say is that middles can be tasty!

Okay, maybe that's enough about sandwiches.

If you're going on a journey, you need to have a map. You need a plan for the trip you're about to take. Same with the hero of your story. She's about to go on a journey to solve her big problem. The journey starts with the problem, and it ends with the solution (aka the resolution, but we'll talk more about that later).

So how does she plan for the trip? She needs to do some or all of the following:

⌖ Gather information
⌖ Decide on a course of action
⌖ Collect tools and supplies
⌖ Find an ally to help her solve the problem

Let's check in with Olivia and Max. Olivia's made it home and is now sitting on the front porch, Max by her side. As we've seen, she has her suspicions that Max originally belonged

to the Schiffers, but she needs to find out if she's right about that. She also wants to know how he ended up in a shelter. It might take her a while to find out whether her suspicions are true, so she needs to hide Max until she can make her case that he belongs to her and with her.

Olivia decides she's definitely going to build a fort in the woods behind her house, where Max will be safe. When she's not spending time with Max in the fort, she'll work on solving the mystery of why Max was in the shelter and who he originally belonged to. She'll start by going to the shelter and asking questions. But the shelter is across town; how will she get there? And how will she get the stuff she needs to build a fort and keep Max comfortable while she's out sleuthing?

She's going to need to ask someone for help—someone who can drive and who can also keep a secret.

How about Evelyn, her brother's geeky ex-girlfriend, who has her driver's license and just happens to love dogs as much as Olivia does?

Worth a shot.

So Olivia has a plan: she's going to hide Max, and solve the mystery of how Max ended up at the shelter and who owned him first.

She's going to build a fort in the woods and then head over to the shelter.

She's going to ask Evelyn, the geeky ex-girlfriend, to drive her around.

What could go wrong?

Okay, another example, because I love examples. Let's say there's a kid named George who likes to keep to himself. He's a reader, a scientist, a philosophical kind of kid, keeps a journal, keeps a clean handkerchief in his back pocket—that sort of guy. Avoids conflict whenever possible. Tries to fly below the radar at all times.

So one day during recess George is out looking for interesting rocks, when he turns the corner of the building and sees Walker Parks, the meanest kid in the seventh grade . . . and Walker Parks is crying. No, not crying—he's sobbing, his face is all red, and there's snot everywhere. George starts tiptoeing backward, because let's face it—Walker Parks is going to smash him like a bug if he realizes George has seen him crying, and George's whole thing is not getting smashed like a bug. . . .

And that's when Walker Parks sees him. "What are you looking at, Fart Brain?" he snarls.

"N-nothing," George stammers. "I was just on my way back to class."

"To tell everyone you saw me crying?" Walker shakes his head. Snorting one last big snort, he tells George, "I don't think so. No, what you're going to do is get me out of this mess."

The mess, it turns out, is that Walker is flunking history, and if he flunks history, his dad won't let him play on the travel hockey team. But if a smart kid like George started writing his papers for him, that would solve the problem—no problem.

And now George has a big problem. Or, as we like to say in this book, a Big Problem.

So what's the plan, George?

The simplest plan is that George could just write Walker's papers for him, doing his best to make them seem Walker-esque—lots of misspelled words, grammatical errors, that sort of thing.

But George is an ethical guy, and besides, he knows if he gets caught, he might get suspended—or worse.

So that plan won't work. Okay, what if George ratted Walker out and told their history teacher about Walker's proposal? That might work—except that we're back to that whole "getting smashed like a bug" thing that George is trying desperately to avoid.

What if . . . well, what if George actually tried to help Walker write his own papers? An uphill battle, sure, but it could be done, and George has always liked a challenge.

"Dude, I'll totally help you," George tells Walker, handing him the clean handkerchief he carries in his back pocket. "But if your papers are going to sound like you wrote them, then you've got to write them."

George suddenly thinks of his uncle Dave's pizza place. Uncle Dave lets him study there, and he'd be cool about letting Walker come, too. Plus, Uncle Dave is a total hockey guy. He and Walker might actually get along.

Uncle Dave would definitely be an ally in this situation.

"We could meet at my uncle's pizza parlor after school," he tells Walker. "It's pretty close by."

Walker looks doubtful. Clearly, he'd rather George just

write the papers for him. Still, he can see that there are benefits to this plan. "Do we get free pizza?"

"All you can eat," George promises. Which isn't technically true—he gets the fifty percent family discount, which isn't the same as free, but George will figure out a way to come up with the money if it means staying alive.

Walker agrees to the idea, and they arrange to meet that afternoon. It's not a bad plan, and it just might work—as long as George can pay for the pizzas. And can figure out a way for Walker to seem smart. And not get smashed like a bug.

Good luck, George!

Best plan? Worst plan? Either way, or somewhere in between, remember the old saying beloved by writers everywhere: keep your hero in trouble. Whatever the plan, don't let it

come off without a hitch! Make sure to throw a banana peel or two on your protagonist's path. You heard it here first, folks: perfectly executed plans are perfectly boring.

THE BIG TAKE-HOME

- ✎ When faced with a big problem, your protagonist needs to come up with a plan for solving it.
- ✎ After your hero comes up with a plan, he needs to collect the information, tools, and supplies he needs to pull his plan off.
- ✎ This plan may not work. Oftentimes, plans have to be redrawn or revised.
- ✎ Sometimes the plan is workable, but it will be difficult to execute. Difficult can be good! Just don't make it so difficult that it's impossible.

WRITERS, START YOUR ENGINES!

1. Brainstorm solutions to your protagonist's big problem. Choose the one that interests you the most.
2. Once you've decided on a solution, work on a plan. What information does your hero need to gather, what tools and supplies? Who are allies who might prove helpful? Make a list.

LET'S WRITE!

Some questions to consider when preparing to write this scene: Does your protagonist come up with a plan right away or does it take a few days? Does she come up with a plan on her own or does she get help from other people (parents, friends, a teacher)? Does she come up with her plan after rejecting several other plans?

Why does she think her plan will work?

What's her state of mind as she's coming up with a plan? Is she excited? Terrified? Stressed? Overconfident?

Where does this scene take place?

Who will be your protagonist's allies as she tries to solve the big problem?

Who will work against her?

As you write this scene, keep in mind what's motivating your protagonist. What's at risk for her if she doesn't solve the big problem?

5

ON THE ROAD, OR STICKS AND STONES

THIS IS OBVIOUS, BUT I'LL GO AHEAD AND SAY IT ANYWAY: if your protagonist's plan goes off without a hitch, your story's going to end up a snooze fest. The sound of snoring you hear in the distance? That would be your reader.

Re-imagine *Hatchet* this way: Brian finds himself stranded on a desert island, but instead of having to struggle to survive, he remembers he has a pack of matches in his pocket. So he builds a signal fire that draws a search plane, and he ends up rescued a few hours after he's stranded.

Gee, what an exciting story!

Yeah, not really.

Miles of smooth highway might make for an easy ride, but it also means somebody's going to be napping in the backseat. What every story needs is a big bump in the road—more than one, as a matter of fact. What every story needs is an interesting and exciting bunch of complications. For our purposes, we'll call these complications **Sticks, Stones, and Monsters**. In this chapter, I'll discuss sticks and stones. We'll give the monsters their own chapter in Chapter Six.

You are familiar with sticks and stones in the real world. You can imagine walking down the road, not really paying attention, and tripping over a stick, getting your feet tangled, and going splat on the sidewalk, right? You can picture riding your bike and hitting a big rock. Wheels go up in the air and so do you. It's happened to all of us.

A story has got to have its sticks and stones—obstacles your protagonist runs into on her journey as she tries to solve her big problem. Some basic true things about sticks and stones include:

Sticks are small problems that are easily solved. They tend to appear at the beginning of the story. Maybe they trip your hero up, but not for long. They're sticks, right? Throw those suckers to the side of the road and keep moving!

Sticks often give your protagonist a false sense of self-confidence. *My path is going to be a smooth one*, she thinks as she easily chucks the stick into the woods, *and all of my problems easily solved*. (Ah, little does she know!)

Funnier, lighter stories often have a lot of sticks in the road. Darker stories might only have one or two before the stones appear.

Stones are boulder-size obstacles. They can be moved off the road, but a lot of times your protagonist will need help pushing them aside. If no help is to be found, your clever hero will find a way to climb over, but he may scrape a knee or sprain an ankle in the process.

As your protagonist journeys down the road, the problems that greet her will get bigger and harder to solve. Early problems are easy problems (sticks), mid-journey problems are more serious (stones).

In our story about Olivia, the first stick in her path might have to do with convincing Evelyn, the big brother's super-smart, super-geeky ex-girlfriend, to give Olivia a ride to the animal shelter. Maybe Evelyn is still unhappy about how Big Brother broke things off. Maybe Olivia was sort of a brat when Evelyn used to come over, and Evelyn hasn't forgotten.

So how does Olivia kick that stick out of the road?

She might offer to pay for gas and buy Evelyn a pizza after

they visit the shelter. (Turns out that Olivia is the kind of kid who never spends her birthday money, so she's got a box stuffed with cash.)

Or she could apologize contritely for being a brat and remind Evelyn of their shared love of all things canine. Olivia remembers that Evelyn has a rescued mutt called Jester. "Do it for Jester," Olivia begs. "Do it for all the good dogs that end up in shelters."

Maybe she asks straight out, "Evelyn, what would it take to get you to drive me to the shelter?" Turns out that Olivia's big brother has taken custody of a game he and Evelyn developed, and Evelyn believes Olivia can help her reclaim what's rightfully hers.

It might be tempting here to have Evelyn play superhard to get, but be careful not to slow down the pace of your story. The first stick or two your protagonist stumbles across should be pretty easy to remove. Save the stones for a little later.

Whatever strategy Olivia decides to use with Evelyn, this is a problem that seems pretty easy to solve. What might a more serious problem look like? What kind of stone might show up in the road and get in Olivia's way?

Let's say that Olivia convinces Evelyn to drive her to the rescue shelter, but when she goes in, no one will give her any information about Max—who his former owner was, when he got dropped off at the shelter or why. Without this information, Olivia's afraid she can't make her case that Max should be hers for good.

This is a boulder-size problem. This is a stone. It's not insurmountable, but it won't be easy. The good news is, Olivia has an **ally** in this situation—Evelyn. Evelyn is a computer girl—a hacker, as a matter of fact—so together they work out a solution for getting around this particular stone. Olivia will make up an emergency to get the person sitting at the front desk out of the way, and while they're gone, Evelyn will hack into the computer and find Max's records. It'll take a few minutes, so Olivia is going to have to come up with a pretty gripping diversion. She's going to have to do a lot of scrambling to get past this stone and on down the road.

If you're wondering how many sticks and stones your story should have, the answer is: it depends.

One, it depends on how long your story is. A short story might have one stick and one stone. A novel is going to have at least a few sticks, and at least two or three stones, maybe more.

Two, it depends on what kind of story you're writing. In some funny stories, the road is littered with sticks and only has one stone. In a more serious story, there might be one stick and several big stones.

I once did a writing workshop where one of the kids wrote about a boy who wakes up as an ant. The writer thought it was going to be a serious story, in which the ant-boy risked annihilation at every turn—which is to say, he thought it was going to be a story with a lot of stones. But as he started writing, he kept coming up with funny stuff about the ant-boy figuring out how to get out of his room (battery-operated toy car), getting downstairs, and almost getting run over by a toddler on a tricycle once he got outside. His story ended up having lots more sticks than stones, and everybody thought it was hilarious.

THE BIG TAKE-HOME

- ∽ Every story has sticks and stones—which is to say, small and not-so-small obstacles that block your protagonist's path.
- ∽ Typically the problems go from smaller to bigger as your protagonist makes her journey. So the first problem or two may be a stick, and then the next problem is a stone.

- When it's time to push a stone aside, sometimes you need a friend, and sometimes you need special skills. What will be true for your protagonist? Who are her allies? What skills does she possess that will help her get the stone out of her way?
- Keep in mind that there should be risk involved in the choices your protagonist makes. She might push the boulder out of the way . . . only to have it roll back over her!

WRITERS, START YOUR ENGINES!

Brainstorm the problems that are likely to confront your hero along her journey. What are three sticks she might run across? What are two stones that might block her path? If you're having trouble coming up with ideas, consider the following:

1. Physical barriers—the road is blocked, the rain is blinding, the bully is standing in between here and there.
2. Emotional barriers—Fear often blocks the way, and anxiety (a subset of fear) can, too. Sometimes sadness can be paralyzing, and sometimes the unwillingness to ruin a good thing can keep your protagonist from chucking that stick into the woods or rolling away that stone.
3. Human barriers—including the usual suspects, by which I mean parents, teachers, and siblings. Also: well-meaning caretakers, concerned police officers, worried friends.

LET'S WRITE!

We've entered the middle of the story. You'll be writing several scenes here, each scene a little more (or a lot more) intense than the scene before it. Imagine your protagonist walking up a hill. It's not that hard at first, but as he continues, the hill gets a little steeper and then steeper still. Turns out that hill was a mountain!

Let's walk through the middle-of-the-story scene-writing thing, and work on some sticks and stones. Follow the following to write your story's next three scenes:

Scene 1: This is a stick scene. Your protagonist has a plan and eagerly gets started. Taking care of that big problem is going to be a piece of cake! Or if not easy, then at the very least doable. So what's the first thing that gets in his way? His teacher keeps him after class to discuss a test, making him late for an important meet-up? Maybe he misses the bus, forgets a book, gets lost on the way to where he needs to go to put his plan in motion. . . . Maybe the friend who's going to help him out of this mess isn't at school.

So what does he do once the stick appears on the path? How does he get past the first obstacle? Is he able to continue with his plan when he does, or does he need to make a change or two? What's he thinking and feeling at this point? If your protagonist started out this scene feeling confident, has his confidence been shaken or does he assume that from this point forward, all will work out just as he planned?

Scene 2: The second stick scene, this one a little bit bigger than the first. Remember that these sticks are obstacles getting in your character's way—they're keeping her from reaching her goal (and her goal is to solve the big problem). You want this stick to be bigger than the first stick, and you also want it to be different from the first stick. If someone keeps running into the same problem over and over, it gets kind of boring.

Scene 3: Write a scene in which your protagonist encounters a stone. What's her reaction? How does she move it out of her way or get around it? Does she need to ask for help? If so, who does she call on?

If your protagonist has a special talent or skill that enables her to move the stone out of the way, make sure this talent or skill has been mentioned earlier in the story so that it doesn't come out of the blue. This is not the time to suddenly reveal that it just so happens your protagonist can fly or do judo.

6

BIG SCARY MONSTERS
& Other Things that Go Bump in the Night

A **MONSTER** IS A MONSTER OF AN OBSTACLE. It's what stands in the middle of the road and threatens to stop your protagonist from reaching the end of his or her journey. It's not a stone that can be pushed off the road or climbed over. The monster has to be confronted head-on and defeated, or else your protagonist's big problem won't be solved.

Monsters come in the form of bullies, storms, sprained ankles, huge misunderstandings, and dangerous rivers that must be crossed. Some monsters might even exist inside of the protagonist. They take the shape of crippling anxiety, fear, grief, self-doubt, or a blind spot the size of the moon.

The monster could also be an actual monster.

No matter what, the monster must be slain.

Before we go any further, let's take a moment to review what's happened in your story so far—what your protagonist has experienced along the road. She's found herself in a situation, and as the result of that situation, she has a big problem.

Olivia has to prove she's her dog's rightful owner, or her dog will be taken from her.

Josh has to figure out how to land safely, or else fall from the sky and get smashed into smithereens.

George has to find a way to help the school's biggest bully without getting beaten up.

So our protagonist comes up with a plan for solving the problem. She sets out on a journey to a land called *Success* or *Problem Solved* or *Everything's All Right Now*.

At the beginning of her journey, there's a stick or two, and she tosses them out of her way. Her confidence remains high. She's got this!

Then she comes across the stone—a big stone. The stone is harder to get around, but with some help from her friends or her own mighty brain, she finds a way—which means she's on her way to victory! She continues down her path, the sun shining brightly, birds singing all around her, everything blue skies and daffodils.

And then the sky darkens, the birds go silent, and our hero screeches to a halt.

Hello, Mr. Monster.

How horrible of you to drop by.

Time for some exampling.

(Yes, *exampling* is a word. You can look it up.)

Remember our pal Josh? The one who woke up one morning and discovered he could fly?

Josh flies outside, and everything is incredible! He's a bird, he's a plane, he's Super Josh! He flies all over town, getting a bird's-eye view on his school and the amusement park, and then heads out to the lake to see what the water looks like from way up high. Amazing!

So what's the big problem? Josh has no idea how to land this plane. Sooner or later he's going to get hungry or tired, and he's definitely going to have to go to the bathroom. A crash landing is out of the question, if Josh wants to live to see another day.

Josh figures that the best thing to do is find some birds to give him a few helpful hints. At the very least, he can watch them fly back to Earth and imitate their moves to the best of his abilities.

Sounds like a plan, Stan. Er, Josh.

Sticks in the road (or, in this case, the sky): The first birds Josh comes across are a trio of blue jays that aren't too happy to see him. They use their beaks like weapons as they try to push him out of their territory. Josh, after a few moments of sheer terror, remembers that he's a lot bigger than a blue jay and scares the birds away by waving his arms around and yelling.

Stones? At first, flying is pretty easy. But when wind kicks up, Josh finds himself flailing about, the air current taking him this way and that. A couple of big gusts send him spiraling toward the Earth. He's pretty sure he's a goner if he doesn't get help quick!

Lucky for Josh, a passing hawk shows him how to work with the wind instead of against it—how to go with the flow, as it were. More confident now, Josh keeps flying. He comes across some swallows that take a friendly interest, so he starts signaling that he's ready to head back down. One of the birds seems to get what he's saying and waves a wing, like, *Follow me, dude, I'll show you!*

You get the picture. Josh kicks away the sticks and rolls away the stones, and everything looks like it's going to be just fine . . .

Until the monster shows up.

The buzzing drone that practically flies into Josh's face is big and has lots of sharp parts . . . and worst of all, it seems to be after him. This midair collision is no accident. The drone wants Josh out of the sky—even if it has to push him out. And down. Way down.

What's the plan now? How will Josh defeat the drone? What will this battle look like?

Will the monster win?

Does your protagonist know who or what the monster is when he hits the road? Sometimes, but not always. Maybe you're writing a story about a boy whose little brother has run away. Let's say he finds his brother deep in the woods, and now his task is to get home safely through a torrential downpour. Their path is blocked by a raging river, and getting across alive seems like a nearly impossible task. The river is the obstacle that must be confronted—it's the monster of the story, one that the boy couldn't have anticipated.

On the other hand, some monsters are clear from the very beginning, or close to it. There's an evil wizard or a big bully. A blizzard has been predicted and is supposed to hit in twenty-four hours.

Interestingly, sometimes the monster is known to the reader but not the protagonist. That's because the monster lives inside the protagonist. Maybe the reader doesn't see this at first, but over the course of the story it becomes clearer: our hero is her own worst enemy.

Which brings us to our old friend Olivia.

Have you ever believed yourself to be right, right, right—only to learn that you were wrong, wrong, wrong?

Perhaps you noticed as we outlined the beginning of Olivia's story that she seems to be a little, well, judgy. A bit too quick to jump to conclusions. We know that she doesn't much like the Schiffer kids, but we don't actually know why, do we? All we know is that Olivia finds them whiny and seems to resent the fact that they live in a nicer house than she does.

Olivia jumps to some pretty fast conclusions when she finds Max in the Schiffers' yard. Once she has the thought that the Schiffers might be Max's first family, she seems to accept it as fact. Moreover, because she doesn't much like the Schiffers, she thinks that Max ended up at the shelter because they didn't take care of him. Even worse, she thinks they might have abused him.

Whoa there, Nelly! Them's some pretty serious charges, based on zero evidence.

That doesn't stop Olivia from going into full detective mode. She's bound and determined to paint the Schiffers as the bad guys so she can get her dog back once and for all. She builds a case against them, and it's a pretty convincing one—at least to Olivia. But what if it turns out to be a case built on top of a sandcastle? What if the Schiffers don't turn out to be the horrible people that Olivia has painted them to be?

What if Olivia turns out to be the horrible one? What if her own prejudices and blind spots keep her from seeing the truth? And here's a really tricky question: How does a girl recognize the monster inside of herself?

THE BIG TAKE-HOME

- ✑ Monsters come in all forms, shapes, and sizes.
- ✑ Sticks and stones can be tossed aside or pushed away, but a monster must always be confronted.
- ✑ Sometimes the monster is in the mirror.

WRITERS, START YOUR ENGINES!

1. Review your story so far.

   Protagonist:

   Situation:

   Big problem:

   Consequences for the protagonist if the problem isn't solved:

   Plan for solving the problem:

   Sticks in the road:

   Stones in the road:

2. Who or what will be the monster obstacle in the road? If you're not sure yet, brainstorm a list of possibilities.

LET'S WRITE!

1. The monster appears on the road. How does your protagonist react? Is the monster expected or unexpected?
2. This might be the time for your protagonist to reflect on what happens if he's defeated in this confrontation. You don't want to slow down the action too much, but you do want to build up the tension. Remember—there's a price to be paid for losing. Make sure it's clear to your protagonist—and your reader—exactly what the cost of losing is in this situation.

The BIG BLOW-UP, aka THE CRISIS POINT

TIME IS UP.

The end is near.

It's the point of no return.

The enemy is almost upon you.

The spell is about to be broken.

The choice must be made.

The river must be crossed.

It all boils down to this.

In the last chapter, we discussed who or what your monster might be. In this chapter we'll talk about the confrontation.

The Hero vs. the Monster.

Whether the monster is an evil wizard out to destroy your protagonist or a river that has to be crossed in order to survive, we've reached the point of the story in which your protagonist either succeeds or fails, all depending on whether the monster is defeated.

She makes it to the other side of the river alive? The monster is defeated!

She drowns while trying to get to the other side? The hero is defeated.

He gets over his fear of heights and climbs to the top of the mountain? The monster is defeated!

He can't make himself climb higher than five feet before dropping back down to the ground? The hero is defeated.

She forces herself to confess that she stole the money, or she spends the money on a new computer game. He musters his courage and asks the girl of his dreams to the dance, or he chickens out and stays home.

Whatever the monster is, if your protagonist slays it, the big problem is solved.

If not?

I think you know the answer to that.

Let's call the point where this confrontation between the protagonist and the monster takes place the **Crisis Point**. Other words and phrases that essentially mean the same thing include *the moment of truth, the turning point, the point of no return, the crossroads*.

This all sounds very dramatic, and in one way or another the crisis point scene *should* be dramatic. Your reader should be on the edge of his or her seat, at least halfway convinced things won't work out, that the monster will win this battle. In fact, at some point it should seem inevitable that the monster will win—the storm will destroy everything, the river will prove too wild to cross, the evil wizard will cast a spell that leaves the hero paralyzed and helpless.

Four things need to happen in the crisis scene:

1. There has to be some sort of buildup—essentially your protagonist has to enter the arena and approach the center of the ring, where the monster awaits.
2. There has to be a struggle.
3. At some point during the struggle, your protagonist needs to be on the brink of losing the fight.
4. There has to be a resolution—win or lose.

One thing you may have noticed in a lot of stories is that the crisis point scene often happens around big events. It's the day of the big race! The big show! The big party! Emotions are running high; there's already a lot of drama and hubbub. This also goes for the last day (of summer, of school) and the day before (the day before the best friend moves, the brother goes to college, the day before the beloved family pet is going to be put to sleep).

Let's look at some of the stories we've been following. What do their crisis points look like?

For Josh the flying boy, the crisis point of his story arrives when a drone comes after him and tries to force him out of the sky.

For Olivia, the crisis point comes when she discovers she

may have been completely wrong about the Schiffers, after spending the last two weeks making sure everyone knows about how they're a bunch of animal abusers.

For George, the crisis point comes when he can't help Walker anymore, and Walker threatens to smash him into smithereens.

Emotions need to be running high at this point in your story. You need to make your reader feel what your protagonist is feeling, whether that's fear, anger, or excitement. Everything turns on this scene, and it needs to be as dramatic as you can make it.

Remember, it all boils down to this moment.

And when this very dramatic moment is over, the big problem has to be resolved. For better or worse, for richer or poorer, your protagonist has walked through the burning building and gotten out the other side.

What does that look like for Josh and Olivia?

Last we saw Josh, he was up in the sky being attacked by a drone (aka the monster). If he doesn't find a way to escape or a means to fight back, he's crash-landing and it won't be pretty. His first instinct is to escape—but how? He's up in the middle of the air, and the drone is much, much faster than he is.

There's only one thing to do, Josh decides, and that's to grab the drone and hold on tight! Either he'll fly or he'll fall, but if he's going down, he's taking the drone with him.

Together, Josh and the drone tumble to the Earth, but because their fall isn't a direct drop, the landing isn't too brutal. When Josh hits the ground, he steadies himself and looks around. He catches sight of a guy standing at the edge of the woods, holding a controller.

It's his dad.

Josh hones in on him like a missile. "What are you doing? Were you trying to kill me?"

"I wasn't trying to kill you," his dad says. "I was testing you. Welcome to the family business, son."

The scene ends here—but not the story. We'll get to the rest of Josh's story in the next chapter. But for now—calamity averted! Crisis resolved. And Josh's big problem, getting down from the sky, is a problem no more.

As for Olivia . . .

For Olivia, the crisis point might come when she runs into the Schiffers' neighbor at the pool and learns the real truth. After Olivia reveals her suspicions that the Schiffers are animal abusers who mistreated

Max before her family took him in, the neighbor sets her straight. The Schiffers may be an unruly bunch, loud and a little obnoxious, but they love dogs and have been taking in dogs from the shelter for years. They weren't Max's first family—they were his first rescue family, and they'd only had him a few weeks before he ran off.

So not only has Olivia been wrong about what happened to Max, she has to accept the fact that she's been wrong about the Schiffers. Worst of all, she's going to have to give Max back.

At first, Olivia refuses to accept the truth. In fact, she has a major poolside hissy fit. The Schiffers aren't great; they're terrible! Max isn't their dog; he's hers! She'll never give him back! She and Max will camp out in the woods forever!

But as the neighbor calmly offers more evidence that the Schiffers are decent and humane humans, the reality sinks in. Olivia realizes she's been wrong about the Schiffers all along. She's been wrong about everything.

In this scene, Olivia confronts a monster made up of her own misunderstandings and her dislike of the Schiffers. These things have blinded her to the truth—that the Schiffers are, in fact, good guys. The scene begins at the pool, where Olivia confronts the Schiffers' neighbor, and it ends with her retrieving Max from the fort and taking him back to the Schiffers' house. The big problem has been resolved—but not in Olivia's favor.

THE BIG TAKE-HOME

- ∽ The crisis point is the confrontation between the protagonist and the monster. Other words and phrases that essentially mean the same thing include *the moment of truth, the turning point, the point of no return, the crossroads.*
- ∽ The crisis point must be dramatic in order to be effective. One way to create drama is to put your protagonist at real risk of losing.
- ∽ By the end of the crisis-point scene, your protagonist's big problem has either been resolved (victory!) or has proven itself unsolvable (defeat!).

WRITERS, START YOUR ENGINES!

1. What are three possible crisis points that will determine your protagonist's fate?
2. What are some of the possible outcomes? Explore

both what victory looks like for your hero and what it would mean for your hero to be defeated.

LET'S WRITE!

1. Have your protagonist approach the monster. Through her actions and reactions, show us how your protagonist feels at this very minute.

2. Describe the confrontation. What weapons does your protagonist use to fight the monster (her wits, her kindness, her physical strength, a big stick)? Is the confrontation physical? Verbal? Both? Who makes the first move? Let the monster get the upper hand at least for a moment.

3. Describe what your character does at the end of this scene. Through her actions and reactions, show rather than tell us how she's feeling.

8

Almost Home
(But You're Not There Yet)!

THE STORM HAS PASSED, the fire has been put out, the enemy has been defeated.

Now what?

You've reached the part of the story where your protagonist is almost home, but not all the way there—let's call it the almost-home scene. Honestly, this can be one of the hardest parts to write. In a way, it feels like the story is already over. What's left to talk about?

Sometimes not much, but usually there are at least a few things that need to be wrapped up, a few loose threads you can't leave hanging.

Let's look at our story about Olivia and Max. When we last saw Olivia, she was carrying Max back to the Schiffers. When she reaches their yard, she gently sets Max on the

grass and says, "You're home now, Max. I'll miss you, but this is for the best."

The end.

No! Not the end.

Okay, this could be the end, if we want everyone to be totally depressed. But if we end the story with Olivia walking home empty-handed, Max whimpering behind her, it feels like something's been left out. The story seems unfinished. We've spent a lot of time with Olivia, and it doesn't seem right just to leave her there crying on the sidewalk. Sure, she was wrong about the Schiffers, but haven't we all been quick to judge at some point or another in our lives?

We need to give Olivia a moment to reflect on what's happened and how she feels about it. She was so sure of herself when the story began, and it turns out a lot of what she thought was true was actually false. Not only that, she's had to say goodbye to her beloved dog. She's heartbroken.

Maybe she needs to sit down for a second.

Olivia sits down on the curb—the same curb she was sitting on near the story's beginning, only now she doesn't have Max in her arms. But as she sits and thinks about what's just happened—the mistakes she made, the loss of her dog—she thinks that the story doesn't have to end this way, with her empty-handed and brokenhearted. Maybe she could knock on the Schiffers' door and explain. Maybe she could ask if she can visit Max from time to time.

She stands up. Instead of walking home, she turns around and heads back to the Schiffers'. *It's worth a shot,* she thinks.

Last we saw Josh, he's just realized that the drone that was trying to take him out of the sky was, in fact, controlled by his father. While ending the scene with Josh's dad saying, "Welcome to the family business!" is a nice dramatic moment, the reader would like a little more explanation, if you please.

In Josh's story, the almost-home scene is where we learn that certain members of Josh's family have been flying since the flying gene entered their DNA sometime in the fourteenth century. For the last six hundred years, they've been airborne spies for kings, queens, emperors, and presidents. Dodging birds and planes was never a problem, but drones? Drones are a new-fangled technology, something the flying family hasn't had to contend with before. Moreover, they come out of nowhere and can bring a flying man down fast.

But not Josh.

Oftentimes, the almost-home scene is a time for resolving unanswered questions. In this case, we learn why Josh can fly and why his dad went after him with a drone. Good things to know! Moreover, the story would have been incomplete without them.

This part of the story—the almost-home part—is also the place in the story where your protagonist's "new normal" is established. Life was one way when the story began, but it's a little (or a lot) different now. The one-time enemy is now a friend, the hated activity (say, having to run a mile every day for P.E.) is now a happily anticipated routine. Sometimes the new normal is a little (or a lot) sad—an ill grandparent has died, a best friend has moved away—but it doesn't mean your protagonist's circumstances are necessarily tragic; just different.

Things that happen on the way to your story's end:

- Someone who's been away comes back.
- Something that's been lost is found.
- Something that has been borrowed is returned.
- If there's been a big storm, the debris is cleaned up.
- A lingering question is answered.
- A small mystery is solved.
- A test is returned.
- News comes from afar.

These aren't major plot points, mind you. If you're writing a mystery, the mystery is resolved either right before the crisis point or during the crisis point. You wouldn't wait until now. However, it's not unusual to have some unanswered questions that are part of the story without being the main point of the story. Maybe throughout, your protagonist has been getting notes in her locker that say, "Don't give up!" or "To make a friend, be a friend," stuff like that. Not a major plot point, just something funny that happens throughout the story. It's only when your protagonist is almost home that she discovers who the author of the notes is (preferably someone unexpected). Loose end wrapped up!

You want to be careful not to overdo the whole "And the moral of this story is . . ." thing here. At the same time, the events of your story will change your protagonist, and you need to show how your protagonist has changed. The greedy kid becomes a little more generous, the timid kid realizes she can be brave when need be. The timid kid might not think, *Wow, I used to be scared of my neighbor Mrs. Grinchly, and now I'm not!* Instead, you might write a scene in which she waves and calls hello to Mrs. Grinchly on her way to tell her best friend everything that just happened to her. The greedy kid doesn't necessarily look in the mirror and think, *I'm not greedy anymore!* What he might do is give his little brother a stuffed animal he knows his brother has always liked a lot. He might note to himself that it wasn't that hard to give something away.

THE BIG TAKE-HOME

- After the crisis point, there are always a few things that need to be wrapped up. These aren't major plot points, but smaller issues that have come up in the story.
- The almost-home scene is often where we see how the events of the story have changed the protagonist. It's better to *show* how the protagonist has changed than to *tell* the reader how the protagonist has changed.
- Avoid giving your story a moral or making it about an important life lesson your protagonist has learned.

WRITERS, START YOUR ENGINES!

1. The big crisis is over, things are settling back down. How's your protagonist feeling right now. Relieved? Sad? Exhilarated? A combination of things?
2. What's the new normal for your protagonist? How has her life changed since the story's opening? What's stayed the same?
3. What needs to be wrapped up? Does your story have any loose ends, any lingering questions? Do we know what's happened to all the major characters?
4. Decide when this section of your story takes place. Immediately after the crisis point? A week later? A year later? Where does it take place?

LET'S WRITE!

1. What is the starting point of the scene? Consider putting your protagonist in action—raking the front yard, working

on a magical potion in the lab, shooting baskets, hauling trash.

2. Consider opening the scene with an observation that indicates we've moved on from the crisis point. ("It was harder to mix potions, now that he was missing two fingers on his left hand.")

3. Try having another character enter the scene. What do the two characters talk about? Maybe the second character brings news or carries an important object that had gone missing.

4. End the scene with your protagonist doing something that shows how the events of the story have changed him.

9

The EXIT RAMP,
aka THE END, aka HOME AT LAST

YOU'VE DONE IT! You've made it to the end of your story! If all has gone well, you've answered The Big What If.

Remember The Big What If? It's what got you started on this journey. *What if a kid woke up one morning and discovered he could fly?*

There wasn't one right answer to that question—there were a million right answers. A million possibilities. But we narrowed it down to this: a kid who discovers he can fly will learn that way up high is an exciting and dangerous place to be. And in the end, he discovers he's inherited the family gift and has a lot more adventures in front of him (and above him).

Now that *you've* answered your own what-if question, you've got one last thing to do: end your story. Please note that the almost-home scene and home-at-last scenes are pretty closely connected. Sometimes they're one and the same. Sometimes the end is just two more sentences at the bottom of the hill toward home.

Olivia's story might end with her knocking on the Schiffers' door. The youngest Schiffer answers, and Olivia points at Max.

"I brought him back," Olivia tells the youngest Schiffer. "I know you guys rescued him first."

"Wally!" the youngest Schiffer exclaims, scooping the dog up and kissing him on the head. "You're finally home."

She looks up at Olivia. "Thanks for bringing him back. I mean, I know you stole him, which was wrong, but you brought him back and that makes everything okay."

"I didn't steal him," Olivia protests. "He was mine. At least I thought he was mine."

A voice calls out from behind the smallest Schiffer. "Who's there, Alice?"

"That girl who stole Wally," Alice calls back. "She brought him home. She says she thought Wally was hers."

"Well, invite her in," the voice says. "Ask her if she likes brownies."

Alice turns to Olivia. "Do you like brownies?"

Olivia nods. "I like brownies a lot."

"Then I guess you better come in," Alice says, and pulls Olivia into the house. "I guess you'll be coming over a lot to visit Wally, so you might as well get used to the place."

That didn't take long, did it?

It could have taken longer, of course. We could have a scene with Olivia sitting at the Schiffers' kitchen table, eating brownies and working out a visitation plan so she can still see Max. That would be fine. But there's enough info in the above scene for your reader to understand that things are going to work out for Olivia, that she and the Schiffers will become friends, and Max/Wally will still be in her life. Nonetheless, if you want a few more moments to firmly establish that scenario, have at it!

The ending is another place you want to avoid the whole "and the moral of this story is" thing. In fact, you should always avoid it, okay? If you've done a good job telling the story, your reader can figure out any morals or lessons on her own. (And keep in mind, very few of us read to learn life lessons—we read because we love a good story!)

So what are some ways to end your story? Consider the following:

∞ End with your protagonist about to embark on a new adventure. ("He picked up his phone and tapped Jack's number. Jack was always talking about wanting to go camping, wasn't he? Well, it was time to start making plans. It was time to go.")

∞ End with your protagonist heading someplace—back home, to school, to a new friend's house. ("She walked toward the bus stop, wondering what it would be like to ride to school without Sarah. *Probably awful,* she thought, but then she remembered what Rosemary said and she changed her mind. Maybe it would be great after all.")

∞ End with your protagonist trying something for the first time. ("He picked up the guitar and strummed it a few times. *Not bad,* he thought. Tomorrow it would sound even better.") Whatever it is, this new activity should tie into the story that's come before it.

Your ending, no matter how brief, should have some connection to the rest of the story. The guy who's ready to go camping may have spent most of the story sticking close to home because his mom's been sick. Let's say that by the end of the story, she finally starts to get better and for the first time in months, the protagonist feels hopeful that things are going to be okay. Going camping seems like a great thing to do now that he doesn't feel like he has to be there in case his mom needs him.

The guy who picks up the guitar may have had to quit playing another instrument earlier in the story, so it's significant that he's found a new instrument he can play. Or maybe he's a perfectionist and won't do anything if he's not sure he'll be great at it. But something happened to him that's made him more willing to take risks.

Things to avoid at the end of a story: cliffhangers, new plot twists, new characters, your protagonist acting in unexpected and unexplained ways. Most importantly, you are forbidden to end a story by saying, "Then she woke up and realized it was all a dream." Absolutely forbidden.

THE BIG TAKE-HOME

∞ Endings don't have to be long scenes. Sometimes the ending of your story emerges from the almost-home scene and only takes a sentence or two.

- ∽ Consider ending your story with your protagonist in action—on her way somewhere, meeting up with a friend, shooting baskets, putting away his magic wand.
- ∽ Make the ending connect with the rest of the story.
- ∽ Avoid ending your story with a cliffhanger or by having your protagonist wake up from a dream.

WRITERS, START YOUR ENGINES!

1. Brainstorm ideas for how you'll end your story. Do you need a whole new scene after the almost-home scene, or is your ending simply the conclusion of that scene?

2. If you're writing a separate scene for the ending, consider where it will take place. Sometimes it can be satisfying to end the story right where it began (although sometimes that's quite impossible). Who will be in the scene besides your protagonist?

LET'S WRITE!

1. What is your protagonist doing at the beginning of the scene?

2. Put your protagonist into action. ("Jeremy picked up the ball."

"Alyssa pulled out the special cloth she used to polish her wand.")

3. Have your protagonist make an observation, to himself or to another character in the scene.

4. End with your protagonist in action. ("He shot the ball into the air and then turned around. He had no idea if it went into the hoop or not." "She put the wand back into its box, where it would wait until she had need of it again.")

After You've Finished
YOUR FIRST DRAFT

YOU'VE BUILT A STORY! You got through the very hard middle part and made it all the way home. Congratulations!

You know you're not actually done, right?

If you find that thought depressing (and most writers do), this would be a good time to remind yourself that all of your favorite books went through several drafts, maybe even as many as a dozen drafts, before they became the books you've read over and over again.

Also keep this in mind: the fact that you need to revise doesn't mean your story is bad. It just means there are ways it could be even better.

So where do you start?

Start by closing your eyes.

Close the file on your computer or put your notebook away for a week—at least. When you've been working hard on a piece of writing, you can lose perspective. Sometimes you finish a story and feel like it's a total failure. But when you read it again a week later, you realize it's pretty good! Unfortunately, the opposite can prove true, too. You love your story when you finish—and then a week later, not so much.

Either way, a week is enough time to allow you to read your story with fresh eyes and see things you didn't see before. You might realize that you left out an important piece of information about your protagonist (She's left-handed! She's scared of dogs!) or you see how you could make the crisis point more dramatic than it already is.

There are several things you can do to self-edit. You can:

- Read your story out loud. You'll catch everything from repeated words to sentences that are kind of confusing or wordy. Try to notice if you start to feel bored at any point of your story. A pretty accurate rule of thumb is that if you're bored, your reader will be bored, too. Maybe all you need to do is cut a sentence or two; maybe you need to rethink the whole scene. What might work better here?
- If you wrote your story in a notebook, type it up. If you typed it, write it in a notebook or type it again in a new document. Again, note places where you feel bored or unenthusiastic.
- Pretend you're pitching your story to a movie producer. Succinctly summarize who your story's protagonist is, his or her big problem, what gets in the way of him or her solving the problem, what the story's crisis point is, and

how the story ends. If you have trouble explaining one part of your story, that might be a sign you need to revise that scene or section.

After you've read over your draft and made changes and additions, it's time to give it to another reader. For many writers, this is the hardest

part of the writing process. It can be painful to have your writing criticized, even when your critic is kind and trying to help. It feels a little bit like walking up to somebody and saying, "Punch me in the gut as hard as you can!"

I mean, who would do that to themselves?

Alas, we all need editors. And while getting feedback on your story might feel like a one-two punch to your solar plexus, it's really not. It's more like getting a shot that pinches a bit, but then makes everything better. (Forget this analogy if the very idea of getting a shot makes you want to faint.)

So how do you find an editor? He or she may be as close as the dinner table. A parent might be happy to help, or a sibling. Other family members work, too. I know one young writer who sends her stories to her grandfather who lives halfway across the country. He's a tough but fair critic, it turns out.

But what if your family members can't bring themselves to be critical (or else find it *waaaay* too easy to criticize)?

You may be lucky enough to have a friend who can be honest about your writing, who can praise what's good as well as point out your story's weak spots and give you great suggestions for revising. If so, lucky you! Unfortunately (or fortunately), our friends oftentimes want to be supportive more than anything, and as a result they find it hard to give negative feedback. But you need the bad news along with the good news, I'm afraid.

One person who might be able to suggest potential editors is your school's media specialist. Media specialists know who the big readers are, and big readers often make the best editors. They've read enough stories to understand how stories work. You could ask your language arts teacher for a recommendation. Language arts teachers also know who the big readers are, and they know who the passionate writers are as well. (Hey, maybe your language arts teacher could help you start a writing group—ever thought about that?)

Even if you can't find an expert editor, ask around—you'll find someone who's willing to read your story and give you feedback if you give them guidelines. At the end of this chapter you'll find a list of questions for editors to consider. You can also use these yourself as you're going over your draft.

Revising is a wash-rinse-repeat kind of deal. The question is, how do you know when you're done? Some writers say you're never really done, that no story is ever perfect, and there's a lot of truth to that. There comes a point where you've done all you can do, and it's time to let go and move on to the next thing.

This brings us to the question of publishing your work. You've reached the place where you've revised several times and nobody (including you) can think of what else you need to change or add to your story. You might be satisfied by a job well done, or you might want to get your story out into the world, give it some readers.

There are a number of ways to do this. You can:

- Submit your story to an online story site for young writers. Try googling "Young Writers' Websites" or "Publications for Young Writers."
- Submit your story to a magazine that publishes young writers' work, such as *Stone Soup*.
- Enter one of Scholastic's writing contests for young writers (artandwriting.org)

I strongly advise you to get a parent or teacher to help you look into publishing opportunities. There are scams out there and less-than-reputable publishers. Please keep in mind that the only time you should pay to have your work published is when you're self-publishing your stories through a reputable online service such as Lulu Press, which will help you design and print great-looking books. You might consider this option after you've written (and revised) four or five stories that you're ready to show to the world. You can share copies with friends and family, and donate a copy to your public library so others can read your wonderful work.

All writers want to be published. We want to share our work. At this stage of your writing career, however, I wouldn't get too hung up on publication. Share your story with friends, show it to a favorite teacher, and send copies to your grandparents. Then get back to work, because you have a new story to write. And another one after that.

QUESTIONS FOR EDITORS TO CONSIDER

Almost anyone who likes to read can serve as a reliable editor. You want someone who knows how to be both honest and kind, and who's willing to go into a bit of detail. Here are some questions that can help you get the constructive feedback you need to revise:

1. Did the opening scene draw you in? If it did, what did you find compelling about this scene? What about it made you want to keep reading? Did you understand what was happening in the opening scene, or were there places were you were confused? How could the writer revise this scene to make it stronger?

2. Did you feel like you understood enough about the protagonist's background and the story's setting for the story to make sense? What other information and details might the author include?

3. Did you read along happily, immersed in the story, or were there places where you had questions or felt more information was needed? Were there scenes that went on too long or needed to go on longer? Did you ever find yourself losing interest?

4. What were your impressions of the protagonist? Did you feel like you understood his or her motivations? How was the protagonist different by the end of the story? Was the change believable?

5. Every story has a big problem that the protagonist must deal with by the end of the story, a conflict that has to be resolved. Was this story's big problem clear? Did the protagonist respond to it in a believable way?

6. What were the obstacles the protagonist had to overcome in order to solve his or her problem? Were the obstacles believable? Did the protagonist overcome them in understandable ways? What suggestions do you have for making these scenes stronger?

7. Comment on the use of specific details throughout the draft. Are there places where more specifics are necessary or would make the writing stronger? Are there places where there's too much detail or too much information?

8. What are your thoughts on the dialogue throughout? Does it sound realistic? Was there any dialogue you felt was unnecessary? Could you tell one character's voice from another's?

9. Was the crisis point—the point in the story where things come to a head—effective? Dramatic? Believable? How could this scene be stronger?

10. Was the ending satisfying? Was it believable? If not, what bothered you about it? Do you have suggestions for how the author could revise the ending?

11. Were there any loose threads at the end of the story? Any questions left unanswered?

11

Here We Are, at the End of the Book, but You'll Be Happy to Know that REALLY IT'S JUST THE BEGINNING

HOW'S THAT FOR THE WORLD'S LONGEST CHAPTER TITLE?

Anyway, here we are, a couple of writers who've just finished writing something. Or at least almost just finished writing something (I still have to finish this chapter). Feels pretty good, doesn't it?

One of the reasons I wanted to write this book was because I talk to so many young writers who have no problem getting started on a story, but can't seem to make it all the way home to the big finish. In my workshops, we follow the plan I've laid out here, and by the time the workshop's over, everyone's super excited because they actually wrote a story from beginning to end. They did it!

And you did it!

Was it easy? Not necessarily. Did you get it perfect the first time? Of course not! But now you know that nobody gets it perfect the first time. You understand that writing is a process, and revision is a part of that process—maybe the most important part of that process.

(Repeat after me ten million times: Writing is a process. Writing is a process. Writing is a process. . . .)

For those of you who really don't like to write, it might be too much to hope that you like it a little better now that you've finished your story . . . but at least you finished! And I bet your story's better than you thought it would be. I bet you're sort of good at this story-writing thing. Maybe you should write another story one of these days. I mean, at least think about it, okay?

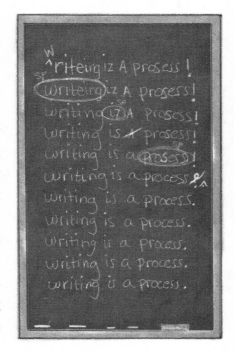

As for the "I Love to Write" writers reading this book, here's my advice to you: Get started on another story immediately! Why? Let me count the reasons. . . .

1. You're all warmed up! Heck, you're on fire! You remember how, way back in the beginning, I talked about writing being like a sport? The more you practice, the better you get. The more you write, the sharper your skills become. If you lay down your pencil for a few weeks, the next time you pick it up you're going to have to warm up again, rebuild your skills, get back into the

rhythm of writing. But if you start a new story right away, you don't even have to stretch. You *are* stretched! Your writing muscles are in great shape.

2. Sometimes when you've written an amazing story (the way you just did), it can be scary to start another one. What if it's not as good as your last story? What if you've peaked as a writer? What if you don't have any good ideas left?

   I've got good news for you: you are pretty much a bottomless well of creativity. As long as you're reading, writing, and observing, you're not going to run out of ideas or inspiration. Does that mean that every idea you come up with will be a winner? Does that mean that all of your stories will be equally as fabulous? No, it does not. You'll write some real stinkers, I promise. But don't worry about it! It's been my experience that every bad story I've written has been followed by a really good one. I don't know why that is, to be honest. But it's made me unafraid to flop. So dust off your pen, open up your laptop, sharpen your pencil . . . and get writing!

3. You're good at this! You've got the gift—and it's the kind of gift you're meant to share. Whatever kind of story you tell next, it's the story somebody is waiting to read. So isn't it time you started writing it?

That's it. That's all my helpful hints, tips, and tricks. That's my big blueprint for putting a story together. Once you get the hang of it, you'll find different ways to write a story. You'll write stories where you start at the end and get around to the beginning. You'll write stories with multiple protagonists and plots. You'll experiment with genres and styles. You'll mess around and discover new ways of telling old tales.

Here's the one thing I ask of you: when you start your stories, do your best to finish them. It's so tempting to give up halfway through, so much fun to begin something new. It can become a habit, not finishing what you start.

My advice: don't give up. Try to stick with a story from start to finish. Nine times out of ten, you'll amaze yourself with what you come up with.

I can't wait to read it.

An Appendix
of Really Useful Hints and Tips

DID YOU KNOW that an appendix is not just a useless organ inside your body?

As it just so happens, the appendix is also the section at the end of a book where the author includes additional info related to the main contents.

So welcome to your appendix!

And no, this is not just a convenient excuse for me to keep blabbering on even though the book is over.

But as long as you're here, I do have a few more things to tell you.

What I've done with this book is given you a blueprint for writing a story.

I haven't focused a ton on the nuts and bolts of writing, because there are great books out there that do that, but not a ton of books devoted to plotting a story. Still, there are a few things I'd love you to know before you go. So get comfy and get reading!

I. SCENES

You've played with building blocks, right? I mean, maybe not since first grade, but you remember what it's like—you put one block next to another until you have a wall, and then you put one block on top of another until you've built a fort or a shopping center or the tallest building ever built by a six-year-old.

A scene is the basic building block of a story. The same way your first grade Empire State Building was made up of individual blocks, every story is made up of individual scenes, one scene after another, each scene moving the story forward until it comes to the end.

Let's break it down.

A scene is a building block.

A scene occurs in one place, in one period of time.

In every scene, something happens and something changes.

Let me repeat this, because it's very, very important: **in every scene, something happens and**

something changes. At the end of each scene, things are at least a little bit different than they were at the beginning of the scene (and sometimes a whole lot different).

Scenes have beginnings and endings. Imagine a director calling, "Action!" to start a scene off and calling, "Cut!" when the scene comes to a close.

Here's an example of what I'm talking about.

ACTION!

Cora sits on the porch of her family's vacation cabin, reading a book and enjoying the beautiful mountain morning. Her dog, Lucky, naps next to her on the porch swing. Everything is quiet except for the birds singing in the treetops.

Shots ring out in the distance. Lucky wakes up and jumps off the swing. He runs into the yard and then toward the woods behind the cabin. Cora throws down her book and chases after him.

After running through the woods for several minutes, Cora stops and looks around. Not only does she not see Lucky, she has no idea where she is. When she looks behind her, she can't see a path. Cora is lost.

CUT!

How do we know this is a complete scene? Something happens—a shot sounds, the dog runs away, and Cora chases after him. Something changes—Cora, who knew exactly where she was in the beginning of the scene, finds herself lost in the woods.

So what happens next?

The next scene, of course!

Some scenes are dramatic—a car chase that ends in an a fiery explosion, for instance, or the last twenty seconds of a close basketball game. In other scenes, the events are less, well, eventful. A new kid shows up in class in the middle of a math test. A ball is hit into a neighbor's yard, the one where the world's meanest dachshund lives. A small thing happens and a small thing changes. Jenna is assigned to show the new kid around and learns they're both trying out for the baseball team next week—and they both play shortstop. Sam hops the neighbor's fence and makes an interesting discovery (there is no dachshund; or there is a dachshund, and there are also dozens of baseballs, footballs, and soccer balls).

Something gets lost. Something is found. A clue is discovered. A body is discovered. Information is uncovered. A secret is told. A lie is revealed. Someone goes away. Someone comes back. A pair of new shoes is ruined. An ankle gets sprained. Something happens. Something changes.

II. CHARACTER STUDIES – HOW TO CREATE REAL PEOPLE IN THE COMFORT OF YOUR VERY OWN HOME!

Write down the names of the first three people you think of, and then make a list of hobbies, interests, personality traits, and characteristics for each person—regular, everyday stuff (good sense of humor; can talk to anyone; likes the Chicago Bulls, the Carolina Panthers, and tacos) as well as information about this person that you consider odd, unique, quirky, or downright weird. Maybe Jackson collects sticks that look like people. Maybe Emma has a YouTube show about fly-fishing. Clyde talks superslow when he's nervous, and Sara blinks superfast when she's excited. Frank only wears purple socks. Marcie hasn't cut her hair in three years.

Everybody's got something going on. Hobbies, obsessions, ticks, tendencies, habits. Even the world's most normal-seeming people have their quirks—and your characters should, too. You don't have to go overboard with this. A little bit of quirkiness can go a long way. Someone can be obsessed with knowing all the songs from all the big broadway hits; that doesn't mean his obsession has to come up in every conversation. But you can mention it once or twice. Real people are really obsessed with *Hamilton* and *Hello, Dolly*, after all. And what you're trying to do here is create characters who are real people.

Hear what I'm saying— not characters *based* on real

people, but characters who *seem* real. Like you could meet them on the bus—or in a dark alley. You wouldn't be surprised to find Mr. Terupt in *Because of Mr. Terupt* walking down your school hallway. You might be surprised to find Dumbledore teaching your science class, but nonetheless, don't you feel like you know him? *Really* know him?

Try the above exercise with each of your story's main characters. What are their hobbies and interests? Their habits and quirks? What mistakes do they make over and over? What are they afraid of? What do people like the most about them?

You want to create characters who make your readers sad to come to the end of your story because they want to spend more time with the people you've created. Well, they may be happy to say goodbye to the bully or the villain—totally understandable. But the rest of the cast? They should be characters your readers know and care about. The real-er you make them, the happier your readers will be.

III. SHOW, DON'T TELL

"Don't tell me the moon is shining; show me the glint
of light on the broken glass."
—ANTON CHEKOV

"Show, Don't Tell" is something that writers hear all the time—but what does it mean?

It's pretty simple, actually. *Olivia was sad about Max running away* is telling. Showing is more like this:

Olivia's throat felt tight and her eyes blurred with tears. Oh, poor Max, *she thought.* He's out there lost and alone!

Another example:

Telling: *There was a full moon.*

Showing: *The moon hung round and shiny as a brand-new quarter in the ink-black sky.*

When you tell something, you're making a statement—the day was cold, the dog was vicious, the test was hard. Your reader might understand what you mean, but he doesn't really *feel* what you mean. Moreover, there are different kinds of cold days. There's the cold day that makes you feel full of energy—a brisk kind of day that feels great once you've moved around a bit—and there's the cold day that will kill you if you stay outside too long. "It was cold" doesn't give any clue as to how cold it was and what effect the cold might have on your characters.

By describing the cold—by *showing* your reader how cold it is—you allow him to see and feel and experience the story as though he himself were in it.

Some great ways to show instead of tell include:

Using Images and Specific Details (more on specific details in just a sec)—"It was a nice day" is boring and doesn't really say anything. "Butterflies floated on a light breeze beneath a cloudless sky" gives us a much clearer picture, as does "It was the sort of day where strangers smiled at each other as they passed on the street, no longer burdened by heavy overcoats and woolen caps."

Making Comparisons—"It felt like," "It sounded like," "It smelled like" . . . Comparisons are a great way to show your reader what your characters are experiencing. Did the music sound awful? You could write "The music sounded like a thousand angry chickens were having choir practice in the attic." Which of these gives a better picture? "Grandpa's hair was sticking up," or "Grandpa's hair looked like it had been styled by a nearsighted Chihuahua"?

You can have a lot of fun with this stuff! "It tasted exactly the way she thought worm stew would taste, like someone had boiled little pieces of shoe leather and bicycle tires in muddy water." "Her skin was as smooth as melted Velveeta." "The afternoon was as cold as a box of Popsicles stored in a freezer inside of an igloo."

Incorporating Body Language—When you're describing how a character feels, using body language can be super effective. Someone's about to give a speech in front of a big audience? You could say, "Bella was nervous," which would be telling, not showing. It gets the point across a lot better if you *show* Bella doing this instead: "As she waited for her turn to give her speech, Bella's damp hands twitched in her lap and sweat trickled down the back of her neck. In spite of the heat, she couldn't stop her teeth from chattering."

When Bella is done with her speech and gets a standing ovation, use body language to show her relief. Instead of saying, "Bella was really happy about how the speech went," you could write something like "Bella skipped back to her seat, waving to her friends and smiling so hard that her face hurt."

If you write, "Jack slumped against the wall and then slowly slid down it, his face as red as an apple," your reader gets the idea that this dude is wiped out by his workout. She might get the same idea if she reads, "Jack was physically exhausted," but she doesn't see Jack's exhaustion or experience it for herself.

IV. SPECIFIC DETAILS – THE WRITER'S BEST FRIEND

Have you ever had that experience where a story seems so real, it feels like you're actually inside of it? It feels so real, it's a shock when your dad calls upstairs that it's time for dinner and you realize you're actually in your house, not the world of the book you're reading. You can't understand how you're supposed to eat when you're taking your potions test at Hogwarts. You don't have time for hamburgers! You've got to solve the mystery of who stole the priceless painting.

How do writers pull you into their worlds like that?

There are at least two ways I can think of—one is by coming up with a plot that keeps your reader turning the pages. (For more about amazing plots, see the rest of this book.) The other is by creating a world that's so vivid that the reader can see it, smell it, and experience it fully. You do that by using specific details—details that help your reader not only see things, but also understand the meaning behind what they're seeing.

For example, "The teacher sat at her desk" doesn't give us much useful information, other than the teacher is in the classroom and she's sitting, not standing. "The teacher sat at her messy desk" tells us a little bit more, but, c'mon, you can do better than that!

"The teacher sat at her desk, which was piled high with ungraded tests and coffee-stained book reports" not only lets us know where the teacher is (sitting at her desk, as opposed to pacing the aisles of the classroom), but it also tells us something about the teacher. She's not the kind of teacher who gets papers returned in a timely fashion. She leaves her coffee cup on top of student papers, which suggests that she doesn't care all that much.

If you really want to give the impression of a teacher who's checked out, you might write, "The teacher sat at her desk and scrolled through her texts, the piles of ungraded tests and coffee-stained student papers blocking her view of the classroom." That doesn't take up much more space on the page than "The teacher sat at her desk," but it tells us a whole lot more about what kind of teacher we're dealing with here!

Through the use of specific details, we learn a lot about this teacher in a very short span of time. If you use them well, specific details will do a lot of heavy lifting for you when it comes to passing along information about your characters, settings, and scenes.

V. TALK THE TALK: SOME TIPS FOR WRITING DECENT DIALOGUE

Dialogue does a lot of important work in a story. It allows characters to exchange ideas, offer information, make discoveries, and express emotions. Dialogue should always have a purpose—even if two characters having a chat seem like they're just shooting the breeze, your characters should never just be talking for the heck of it. Their conversation should be revealing in some way—we should discover some new info or gain some fresh understanding of at least one of the speakers. *Whatever* your characters are gabbing about, their dialogue should move your story forward.

The trick with writing good dialogue is to make it sound real, but not too real. Real conversations between people can be full of *ums*, *likes*, and *you knows*, long pauses, and lots of asides and tangents. It can take real people five minutes or five hours to get to the point, but your characters don't have that kind of time.

In general, people use contractions when they speak—*I'm* instead of *I am*, *couldn't* instead of *could not*, *wasn't* instead of *was not*. Have your characters do the same, unless they're speaking very formally or trying to emphasize the seriousness of a situation. (There are probably a few more exceptions to this rule, but you get my drift.)

After you've written a section of dialogue, read it out loud. Rule of thumb: if the dialogue sounds awkward or stiff as you read it, it will sound awkward or stiff to your reader as she reads it to herself. If you trip over words, it means the words aren't right or there are too many of them.

Make sure a character's vocabulary matches her age and personality. The words your characters use shine a light on who they are.

VI. OKAY, I'M DONE

AND THIS TIME I MEAN IT. THAT'S RIGHT: THIS IS THE END OF THE APPENDIX.

NOW:

THE END . . . OR, MAYBE . . .
THE BEGINNING?

ACKNOWLEDGMENTS

I DEDICATED THIS BOOK to Caitlyn Dlouhy, my editor of more than twenty years, who I like so much I'm going to acknowledge her as well. I won't say Caitlyn taught me all I know about writing stories, but she certainly taught me all I know about writing stories that people actually want to read. Thanks for everything, Chief! Thanks goes to Alex Borbolla, who helped make so many things about this book better (especially the funny bits); to Jeannie Ng, who makes everything right; and to Justin Chanda, the best publisher a girl could have. A big shout-out to Charlotte Vollins and Ellie Crews, aka my writing group girls, who have made me a better teacher. To the fifth-grade students of Glenwood Elementary School in Chapel Hill, North Carolina, (who will be sixth graders by the time this comes out) and their awesome teachers—Elizabeth Angell, Janine Barr, and Linda Keller—thanks for being my guinea pigs! Thanks to Kristin Esser, for her enthusiasm about this project and all of the others.

Thanks to Stacy Ebert, whose illustrations fill me with joy.

As always, thanks to my family, whose support is endless, and to Travis, who is a good dog.

—F. O. D.